MARIE-PIERRE MOINE'S FRENCH KITCHEN

CHICKEN AND OTHER POULTRY DISHES

LES POULETS ET VOLAILLES

ILLUSTRATED BY NADINE WICKENDEN

PAVILION

For Françoise Moine

First published in Great Britain in 1994 by
PAVILION BOOKS LIMITED
26 Upper Ground, London SE1 9PD

Designed by Andrew Barron & Collis Clements Associates

A CIP catalogue record for this book is available
from the British Library
ISBN 1-85793-2129

Text set in Garamond Simoncini with Futura Book and Bold detailing.

Printed and bound in Italy by New Interlitho
2 4 6 8 10 9 7 5 3 1

This book may be ordered by post direct from the publisher.
Please contact the Marketing Department.
But try your bookshop first.

CONTENTS

INTRODUCTION

Wherever you are in France, if you leave the motorway and drive a few kilometres, you will soon come into a village that looks dead to the world. Not a soul about, shuttered windows, faded circus posters on peeling walls. Only when you start listening will the place come to life – a church bell, perhaps, or a ragged rehearsing brass band, more likely, dogs barking and – certainly – poultry clucking in some backyard. If you are in luck, the local rooster may serenade a proud welcome. After all, *le coq* is a well established national symbol.

Poultry has a very special place in the French kitchen. In the old days, when each farmhouse had to be self-sufficient, it was the most widely available source of animal protein. When resources were scarce and the diet meagre, birds from the courtyard were reserved for high days and holidays. With a little ingenuity, vegetables from the *potager*, mushrooms from the forest, a handful of *fines herbes*, and a slug of wine from the cellar, the toughest old hens soon turned into a feast.

The days of rural economy are long gone but French poultry has survived the population exodus to the big cities and the realities of mass marketing. The techniques acquired over the centuries to make the best of what's available are just as effective with the bland prepacked and portioned poultry from the supermarket cabinet as they once were with the wily aged survivors of barnyard feuds and pot-shots.

At the gourmet end of the market, poultry for special occasions and *haute cuisine*, the French love of good food and talent for protectionism has kept standards very high with strict breeding and feeding regulations, and rigorous quality control.

Chicken is France's favourite bird. Like wines, they have their *appellations*, often called *labels*. The white fleshed chickens of Bresse, in the centre-east of the country, are the most celebrated, but they are faced with ever-increasing competition. Again, as with wines, people tend to prefer their local heroes and they support and publicize the best home-grown chickens of their region – yellow maize-fed birds in the Landes, black chickens with more colour in their flesh elsewhere in the south west, pale tender chickens near Le Mans.

POULETS

CHICKEN

POULET ROTI

ROAST CHICKEN

Serves 4 to 5

*1 corn-fed or free range
chicken weighing about
1.5 kg/3 ½ lb, wiped clean
and at room temperature
1 tsp dried rosemary or
tarragon
2 tbsp olive oil
30 g/1 oz soft butter
4 tbsp dry white wine
3 tbsp chicken stock (or
water mixed with a few
drops of soy sauce)
2 tbsp cream or 15 g/½ oz
chilled diced butter, to finish
the sauce
sea salt and freshly ground
black pepper*

Poulet rôti is a universal French favourite. It is the dish grandparents ritually serve visiting grandchildren, with *pommes frites*, chips or *purée de pommes de terre*, creamed potatoes. And somehow it remains a simple treat for the rest of many people's lives, one that never fails to bring back happy memories.

Chicken for roasting is bought carefully, often ordered in advance from the shop or even the farm. It should be plump to stay moist during cooking and brought to room temperature before you put it in the oven. In classic French cooking, very little is done to enhance the bird's texture and flavour. In summer, however, *fines herbes*, aromatic herbs from the garden, are used liberally. If you have fresh tarragon, insert a few sprigs in the cavity as well as between the skin and the flesh for added fragrance, and use 1 or 2 tablespoons of crème fraîche to finish the sauce.

★   Heat the oven to 200°C/400°F/Gas 6. In a cup, mix the dried rosemary with the oil. Season generously.

Lightly season the chicken cavity, then place the chicken on a rack in a roasting tin and lightly season the outside. Pour a small glass of water into the tin. Spoon the seasoned oil over the chicken. Cut the butter into 4 small knobs and dot these over the bird. Season again.

Roast, breast-side up for 20 minutes, then turn the chicken over and roast for a further 30 minutes. Turn the chicken back to breast-side up, baste well with the cooking juices and roast for a further 20 minutes. Continue basting a few times during cooking.

Before you turn off the oven, push a skewer into the thickest part of the inside of the leg to make sure that the cooking juices are clear and the chicken is thoroughly cooked. Leave the chicken to settle for 10 minutes in the switched off oven with the door closed.

Drain the cavity juices into the tin. Place the bird on a carving board and, if possible, get someone to carve the chicken while you make the sauce. If the juices are very greasy, skim off some of the surface fat. Place the tin over high heat and pour in the wine. Boil until reduced by a third, then add the stock or water and stir until bubbling. If you are carving yourself, reduce the heat and keep gently simmering while slicing the bird.

When you are ready to serve, adjust the seasoning. Moisten the chicken with 2 or 3 spoonfuls of the simmering sauce. Whisk the cream or butter into the tin, to thicken and gloss the sauce. Strain into a small heated sauce boat. Serve as soon as possible.

POULE AU POT FARCIE

STUFFED CHICKEN IN THE POT

Serves 6

*1 large corn-fed chicken,
with its liver for the stuffing
1 small cabbage
450 g/1 lb carrots, scraped
and cut into segments
450 g/1 lb mixed small new
potatoes and turnips, scraped
and halved
a small head of celery,
washed, trimmed and cut
into segments
several sprigs of parsley
2 bay leaves
1 tsp dried ground thyme
sea salt and freshly ground
black pepper*

For the stuffing:

*100 g/4 oz smoked bacon,
cut into pieces
100 g/4 oz cooked ham, cut
into pieces
2 tbsp breadcrumbs made
from 2-day-old bread
2 cloves garlic
1 egg
1 tsp dried rubbed sage
sea salt and freshly ground
black pepper*

T his traditional dish comes from the south west of France where it has featured on tables for high days and holidays for hundreds of years. The gutsy vinaigrette is named after the town of Sorges in the Périgord. To enjoy this dish as the locals do, serve it in wide soup or pudding bowls. Ladle the stock over pieces of toasted bread and eat as a first course before the chicken.

★ Prepare the stuffing. In the food processor whizz together the chicken liver, bacon and ham with the breadcrumbs, garlic and

sage. Scrape the mixture from the sides of the bowl, add the egg and season lightly.

Spoon the stuffing into the chicken cavity. Secure the opening with a needle and cotton and with skewers. Put the chicken in a stock pot or very large heavy-based saucepan. Cover with water and very slowly bring to a boil over low heat, skimming the surface when necessary.

As soon as the water bubbles, add the vegetables and herbs to the pot. Season. Bring back to a moderate simmer and cook gently for $1\frac{1}{4}$ to $1\frac{1}{2}$ hours, skimming a few times and keeping the heat low.

Make the *Sauce Sorges*. In a jug, whisk the oil and vinegar together. Spoon in the egg yolk and whisk again. Stir in the remaining ingredients. Using a ladle, poach the egg white in the simmering stock for a minute or two until firmly set. Chop up and whisk into the sauce with 2 tablespoons of stock. Season to taste.

To serve, remove the chicken and vegetables from the pot. Arrange attractively on a warm platter, moisten with a little liquid and remove the cotton and skewers. Keep warm. Discard the seasonings and serve the broth as a first course, then serve the chicken with the *Sauce Sorges*.

For the Sauce Sorges:

*6 tbsp groundnut or
sunflower oil
$1\frac{1}{2}$ tbsp red wine vinegar
1 egg, separated
$\frac{1}{4}$ tsp Dijon mustard
1 tbsp each finely snipped
parsley and chives
1 shallot, finely chopped*

POULET A L'AIL

CHICKEN POT-ROASTED ON A BED OF GARLIC

Serves 4 to 5

1 free range or corn-fed chicken, wiped and ready to cook
2 to 3 tbsp fruity olive oil
45 g/1½ oz butter
250 ml/8 fl oz light chicken stock
a few sprigs each of fresh coriander and parsley, and 1 tbsp finely snipped parsley, for the sauce
finely grated zest and juice of ½ unwaxed lemon
4 to 5 heads of very fresh garlic
sea salt and freshly ground black pepper

The amount of garlic used in this Provençal recipe may seem excessive but the flavourful purée will be thoroughly cooked and free of odorous pungency by the time the chicken is ready. Use very fresh garlic. If you are not sure of its freshness, first blanch the heads in boiling water for 5 minutes before adding them to the stock. I sometimes add cream rather than olive oil and butter to the garlic purée.

★   Heat the oven to 220°C/425°F/Gas 7. Lightly season the cavity of the chicken. Put half the olive oil and half the butter in a large deep flame-proof cooking pot or roasting tin. Place over moderate heat, then add the chicken and brown lightly on all sides.

Lift the chicken from the pot, pour in the stock and bring to a simmer, with the herbs, lemon juice and zest and heads of garlic. Put the chicken on top of the garlic. Dot with a quarter of the remaining butter and season well. Cover tightly with a double layer of foil.

Put the pot or tin in the oven and cook for 1 hour. Remove the foil and baste the chicken well with the cooking liquid. Adjust the seasoning and return to the oven, uncovered, for 15 to 20 minutes, until golden and cooked through.

Lift the chicken from the pot or tin, put in a heat-proof dish and return to the switched off oven for 10 minutes. While the chicken is settling, strain the cooking liquid into a saucepan, bring to a simmer and allow to bubble gently until a little thickened. Reserve the garlic.

As soon as the heads of garlic are cool enough to handle, separate out the cloves. Have a small saucepan ready. Squeeze each clove between your thumb and index finger to extract the pulp and drop this into the saucepan. Season lightly. Beat in the rest of the olive oil (add a little extra oil, if you like) with a small piece of butter and heat through gently.

Adjust the seasoning of the cooking liquid and keep warm until ready to serve. Carve the chicken. Stir the lemon juice, snipped parsley and reserved butter into the cooking liquid. Moisten the chicken with a few tablespoons of this sauce and pour the rest into a heated sauce boat. Spoon the garlic purée into a small heated bowl. Serve as soon as possible.

POULE AU POT

POACHED CHICKEN

Serves 4

1 large corn-fed chicken
1 bouquet garni
6 peppercorns
a pinch of fennel seeds
450 g/1 lb young carrots
450 g/1 lb small leeks
450 g/1 lb baby turnips
450 g/1 lb new potatoes
240 g/8 oz frozen broad
beans
a few sprigs of parsley and
chervil, snipped
sea salt and freshly ground
black pepper

For the mayonnaise verte:

250 ml/8 fl oz mayonnaise
1 clove garlic, crushed
1 tbsp coarse-grain mustard
1 tbsp finely snipped parsley
1 tbsp finely snipped spring
onion

A lighter version of *Poule au pot farcie* and a great one-pot meal.

★   Prepare the stock. Cut off the chicken wings. In a large pot, bring about 1.8 l/3¼ pt water to the boil. Add the chicken wings, bouquet garni, peppercorns and fennel seeds. Chop up one of the carrots, one of the leeks and one baby turnip and add these to the pot. Season. Return to the boil, then reduce the heat a little and simmer for 15 to 20 minutes.

Add the chicken to the pot and bring back to a simmer. Cook gently for about 1 hour, keeping an eye on the heat, until the chicken is cooked through and the juices run clear.

Prepare the mayonnaise while the chicken is simmering. Lightly whisk in the garlic then the mustard. Stir in the parsley and spring onion. Adjust the seasoning – the mayonnaise should be well seasoned. Cover and chill until needed.

After simmering the chicken for about 40 minutes, start cooking the vegetables. First add the potatoes to the pot. Bring back to a simmer, then 5 minutes later drop in the carrots and turnips. A few minutes later add the leeks then the broad beans. Simmer until the vegetables are cooked but still firm – they will go on cooking a little after you take them off the heat.

Lift the chicken from the pot and drain. Leave to cool a little, then remove the skin before serving. Place on a warmed serving platter.

Now place a colander over a large jug bowl or bowl. Tip in the stock and vegetables. Leave to cool until you can handle.

Discard the seasonings and chopped cooking vegetables.

To serve, arrange the vegetables in attractive heaps around the chicken. Moisten with a little hot stock and sprinkle with plenty of herbs. Serve with the jug of hot stock and with the *mayonnaise verte* in a warmed jug.

COQUELETS FARCIS

STUFFED POUSSINS

Serves 2 to 4

*2 plump poussins, wiped and
ready to cook
1½ tbsp groundnut or
sunflower oil
60 g/2 oz butter, diced
2 chicken livers, rinsed
1 tbsp chopped hazelnuts
2 heaped tbsp small pieces of
day-old bread, crust removed
½ tsp each dried ground
thyme and rubbed sage
3 tbsp brandy
2 tbsp crème fraîche
1 small egg
6 tbsp dry white wine
1 tbsp orange marmalade or
blackcurrant jelly
sea salt and freshly ground
black pepper*

The best poussins I ever cooked were Cornish hens and came from an organic market in Chicago. They were plump and succulent. A delicate stuffing turned them into truly festive birds for *le dîner du réveillon* (Christmas Eve supper), at my sister's last year – a genuine French meal I had fun preparing with splendid American ingredients. Serve, like we did, with sautéed mushrooms and small *haricots verts*. Allow one poussin per person for hearty appetites, half otherwise.

★ Lightly season the cavity and the outside of each poussin. Prepare the stuffing. In a small frying pan, heat 2 teaspoons of oil and a little of the diced butter.

Sauté the chicken livers over a moderate heat for 1 to 2 minutes until just firm and coloured. Leave to cool for a moment, then chop and put in the bowl of the food processor. Whizz for a few seconds, then add the chopped hazelnuts, bread, herbs, and a tablespoon each of brandy and crème fraîche. Whizz for a few seconds, then scrape from the sides of the bowl and whizz in the egg.

Heat the oven to 200°C/400°F/Gas 6. Spoon half the stuffing into the cavity of each poussin. Secure with a skewer. Coat the base of a small roasting tin with the rest of the oil. Add the poussins, breast-side down, and dot them with half of the butter.

Roast for about 20 minutes, then turn the poussins breast-side up, baste well with the cooking juices and a few tablespoons of boiling water. Continue roasting for a further 20 minutes. Baste again and reduce the oven temperature to 180°C/350°F/Gas 4, or the next notch down if your oven is very hot. Roast for another 20 to 30 minutes, until the poussins are cooked through, basting once or twice.

Sprinkle the poussins with the rest of the brandy and set alight with a long match. After the (modest) flames have died down, strain the cooking juices into a small saucepan. Return the poussins to the switched off warm oven while you finish the sauce.

Add the wine and the marmalade or jelly to the saucepan and bring to a simmer. Simmer over moderate heat for 2 to 3 minutes, then whisk in the rest of the crème fraîche. Adjust the seasoning. When ready to serve, whisk in the butter and dribble the sauce over the poussins. Serve at once.

POULETS EN MORCEAUX

CHICKEN PIECES

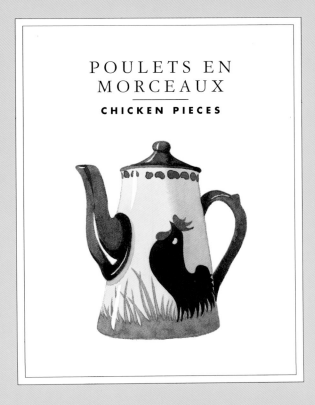

FRICASSEE DE POULET AU VIN BLANC

SAUTEED CHICKEN WITH WHITE WINE

Serves 4

1 small chicken, jointed or
6 chicken pieces
1 tbsp groundnut or
sunflower oil
30 g/1 oz butter
white parts of 3 large spring
onions, chopped
2 slices smoky bacon,
chopped and blanched
1 shallot, chopped
½ tsp dried rubbed thyme
1½ tbsp finely snipped fresh
parsley (or parsley and
chervil)
2 tsp finely grated zest and
2 tbsp juice from an
unwaxed lemon
100 ml/4 fl oz dry or
medium dry white wine
100 ml/4 fl oz chicken stock
5 tbsp crème fraîche, soured
or single cream
1 large egg yolk (or 2 small
yolks)
sea salt and freshly ground
black pepper

This recipe comes from the Anjou-Touraine region of the western Loire where there is barnyard poultry and white wine in abundance.

★   In a sauté pan, heat the oil and butter. Over low heat, sauté the onions, bacon and shallot for a few minutes until softened and a little coloured, then push to the sides and add the chicken pieces. Sauté until they are lightly browned, turning the pieces over to colour them evenly.

Season lightly and sprinkle in the thyme, half the fresh herbs and the lemon zest. Moisten with the white wine, stir and bring to a simmer, then cover partly and cook over a moderate heat until the chicken is cooked and the liquid well reduced – about 30 minutes. Stir from time to time during cooking and reduce the heat if the mixture is simmering too fast.

Pour in the cream and stir until heated through. Now lift the chicken from the pan with a slotted spoon. Keep warm on a heated serving dish.

In a cup mix the lemon juice with the egg yolk. Spoon in 3 tablespoons of the hot sauce from the pan. Stir until the *liaison* is smooth.

Whisk the egg mixture into the pan. Adjust the seasoning and spoon the sauce over the chicken. Sprinkle over the rest of the fresh herbs and serve immediately.

POULET SAUTE AU VINAIGRE

CHICKEN WITH A VINEGAR SAUCE

Chicken and wine vinegar mix happily in the sauté pan, with a pleasing *soupçon* of sharpness. Tarragon is an optional extra which I like using in my version of this classic French dish.

★ Heat the oil and one third of the butter in a large sauté pan. Add the chicken with the shallot, season and sauté for several minutes over moderate heat, turning the pieces so that they colour lightly and evenly.

Reduce the heat to low and sprinkle over 2 tablespoons each of vinegar and stock or water and soy sauce. Cover and cook very gently for about 30 to 35 minutes, until the chicken is cooked through. Keep the heat low so that the chicken remains tender, turning over the pieces once or twice and shaking the pan several times during the cooking.

When the chicken is cooked, lift it from the pan and keep it warm on a heated serving dish. Pour the rest of the vinegar in the pan, stir in the crème fraîche and, if you like, snip in a few tarragon leaves. Stir in the rest of the stock or water and soy sauce and adjust the seasoning.

Stir for a minute over moderate heat, then whisk in the rest of the butter. Spoon the sauce over the chicken, snip over a little more tarragon, if you like, and serve immediately.

Serves 4

*4 boned and skinned
chicken breasts
2 tsp groundnut or
sunflower oil
45 g/1½ oz chilled diced
butter
1 shallot, finely chopped
4 tbsp white wine vinegar
6 tbsp chicken stock (or
water mixed with 1 tsp light
soy sauce)
1 or 2 sprigs of fresh
tarragon (optional)
4 tbsp crème fraîche, Greek-
style yogurt or low fat crème
fraîche
sea salt and freshly ground
black pepper*

POULET AUX HERBES DE PROVENCE

AROMATIC BAKED CHICKEN LEGS

Serves 4

*4 chicken legs or 8 chicken
drumsticks
sea salt and freshly ground
black pepper*

For the marinade:

*2 cloves garlic, crushed
2 tbsp olive oil
1 tbsp hot coarse grain
mustard
1 tbsp crème fraîche or
cream cheese
4 tbsp dry white wine or
2 tbsp lemon juice mixed
with 2 tbsp water
2 tsp honey
1 tsp each dried ground
thyme, rosemary, summer
savoury, marjoram or
oregano
a pinch of cayenne*

This easy-to-prepare chicken dish is full of gutsy Mediter-ranean flavours. Serve with sauté potatoes, a green leaf salad and drink with it a glass of dry rosé wine. Allow an extra 10 to 15 minutes' cooking time if you use leg portions rather than drumsticks.

★   In a shallow bowl, mix the marinade ingredients. Using a sharp knife, score the chicken pieces in several places, going through the skin into the flesh.

One by one, dip the chicken pieces in the marinade until well coated. Put them in a single layer in a gratin dish or roasting tin. Scrape any marinade from the bowl and spoon over the chicken. Cover and refrigerate overnight or for at least 1 hour.

Heat the oven to 200°C/400°F/Gas 6. Season the chicken and put in the oven. Bake for about 35 to 40 minutes, then turn down the heat to 170°C/325°F/Gas 3 and continue cooking for 20 to 30 minutes until the chicken is cooked through. Leave to settle in the turned off oven for 10 minutes before serving straight from the dish.

BROCHETTES DE POULET ET DE FOIES DE VOLAILLE

CHICKEN AND CHICKEN LIVER SKEWERS

These quick *brochettes* are delicious on a bed of very lightly dressed mixed green salad – the marinade will moisten the leaves. Eat while the *brochettes* are still piping hot.

★   Prepare the ingredients. Cut the chicken into 3 cm/1¼ in cubes, cut each bacon slice into 3 segments and roll up 8 of the segments. Cut each chicken liver in half. Roll the rest of the bacon around the liver.

In a shallow bowl, mix the olive oil, garlic, dried herbs and grated zest. Season generously. Thread the chicken, liver and bacon on to 8 skewers. Add to the marinade and toss to coat. Leave in a cool place for 20 to 30 minutes.

Heat the grill to hot. Reserve the marinade and use to baste the skewers.

Reduce the heat a little and grill for 8 to 10 minutes, turning the skewers over 2 to 3 times during cooking and basting them with the marinade.

Just before serving, sharpen the *brochettes* with a sprinkling of lemon juice. Adjust the seasoning and serve immediately with the marinade.

Serves 4

240 g/8 oz boned and skinned chicken breast
4 thin slices of smoked bacon, blanched
2 chicken livers
3 tbsp olive oil
1 clove garlic, crushed
½ tsp each dried sage and marjoram
¼ tsp finely grated unwaxed orange zest
½ tsp each finely grated unwaxed lemon zest and
1 tbsp lemon juice
sea salt and freshly ground black pepper

COQ AU VIN

CHICKEN COOKED IN RED WINE

Serves 4

*4 tsp groundnut or
sunflower oil
60 g/2 oz chilled butter diced
100 g/4 oz rindless smoky
bacon, chopped and blanched
white parts of 8 round
spring onions
2 shallots, finely chopped
1 jointed chicken or 6 to 8
assorted chicken pieces
4 tbsp brandy
1 tbsp flour
1 bottle red wine
1 bouquet garni
30 g/1 oz bitter chocolate,
chopped or grated
240 g/8 oz button
mushrooms, wiped and
thinly sliced
sea salt and freshly ground
black pepper*

Much of French home cooking is based on an appealing balance of thrift and *gourmandise*, an enthusiasm for good eating. When faced with the problem of making a tough rooster, past its prime, taste palatable, farmers' wives of old used a bottle of red wine, plenty of flavourings and let the cooking pot, the black cast-iron *cocotte,* slowly work its magic on the old bird – *coq au vin* was born. What started as a way to deal with ageing cockerels has become a classic, perhaps the best known of French chicken casseroles. For the dish to be as it should be – darkly delicious – it has to be cooked over low heat with robust red wine (not with a mixture of wine and water), left to marinate for several hours and gently reheated.

★　Heat half the oil and one-third of the butter in a large sauté pan over moderate heat. Sauté the bacon, onions and shallots until lightly coloured. Push to the sides of the pan and add the chicken. Season and sauté the pieces until golden, turning them over so that they colour evenly.

Spoon over the brandy and carefully set alight with a long match. Once the flames have stopped, sprinkle over the flour and stir in well. Pour in the wine, add the bouquet garni and the chocolate, and bring to a simmer, over low to moderate heat.

Cover and reduce the heat. Cook for 40 minutes or until the chicken is cooked through and tender. Take off the heat, leave to get cold and marinate for a few hours (or overnight in a cool place).

About 20 to 30 minutes before serving, place the pot over low heat. Gently reheat the chicken, still covered. As soon as the chicken is nearing simmering point, heat the rest of the oil with half the remaining butter in a small frying pan. Sauté the mushrooms over moderate heat for 3 to 5 minutes until tender. Drain on a double layer of paper towels. Season the mushrooms and add them to the pot.

Reduce the sauce a little before serving. Lift the chicken pieces, onions and mushrooms from the pot and keep warm on a heated serving dish. Discard the bouquet garni.

Turn up the heat, bring to the boil and thicken the sauce a little, stirring well. Whisk in the rest of the butter, then adjust the seasoning, spoon over the chicken and serve at once.

POULET EN TAJINE

POT-ROASTED CHICKEN WITH RAISINS AND SPICES

Serves 4

4 chicken portions
2 tbsp olive oil
1 sweet large white onion,
finely chopped
1 to 2 cloves garlic, crushed
1 generous tsp grated fresh
ginger root
pinch of saffron
½ tsp cumin
½ tsp paprika
¼ tsp harissa or chilli paste
2 tbsp slivered almonds
1 tbsp raisins
300 g/10 oz carrots, peeled
and cut into chunks
300 g/10 oz baby turnips,
peeled and halved
4 spring onions
sea salt and freshly ground
black pepper

Some of the spices, techniques and utensils of France's North African past have been adopted into the country's culinary repertoire. A *tajine* is a round earthenware cooking pot with a conical lid – a perfect medium for slow cooking.

This dish is best accompanied by bulgur or couscous.

★ Bring a kettle to the boil. Lightly season the chicken pieces. Heat half the oil in a frying pan and sauté the onion and garlic for 2 to 3 minutes over moderate heat, stirring frequently.

Spoon the mixture into a cooking pot. Sprinkle with the spices, almonds and raisins. Stir well. Put the chicken pieces on top of the mixture. Add the vegetables. Season again lightly.

Pour in enough boiling water to half-cover the chicken and vegetables. Bring to a simmer over moderate heat. Reduce the heat, cover tightly and cook gently for about 45 to 50 minutes until the chicken is cooked through.

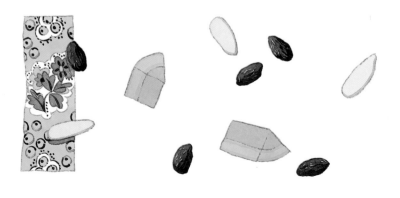

Heat the rest of the oil in the frying pan. Lift the chicken and the vegetables from the pot, allowing the juices to drip back into the cooking liquid. Pat the chicken dry with paper towels, then sauté it over moderate heat in the frying pan until lightly coloured. Keep the vegetables warm.

Meanwhile, turn up the heat under the pot and boil the cooking liquid to reduce for a few minutes – until you have about 1 l/1³/₄ pt of stock. Adjust the seasoning. Skim off excess surface fat.

To serve, return the browned chicken and the vegetables to the pot. Use some of the cooking liquid to moisten the bulgur or couscous.

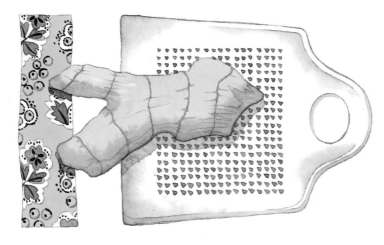

BLANCS DE POULET A L'INDIENNE

CHICKEN-BREAST FILLETS WITH SPICES AND CREAMY SAUCE

Serves 4

*4 boned and skinned
chicken breasts
1 tbsp groundnut or
sunflower oil
½ Spanish onion, finely
chopped
2 tsp flour
2 cloves garlic, crushed
¼ tsp chilli paste
½ tsp ground coriander
½ tsp ground cumin
½ tsp grated fresh ginger or
ground dried ginger
pinch of ground saffron
2 generous tbsp crème
fraîche or Greek-style yogurt
a few leaves of fresh
coriander (optional)
sea salt and freshly ground
black pepper*

I'd like to think that perhaps it is because France's relationship with India was less intense and intimate than England's, that fiery hot spices are less popular *chez nous* than gentler mixes in dishes *à l'indienne*. . . Serve this mildly spicy dish with plain rice cooked with a handful of pine nuts and raisins.

★　Heat the oil in a large sauté pan. Sauté the chicken and onion in the pan over a moderate heat for a few minutes, season lightly and turn the pieces so that they colour evenly.

Sprinkle in the flour, then stir in the garlic. Cook for a minute, stirring well, then sprinkle in the spices. Heat through for a minute or two, mixing the spices well into the chicken and onion. Pour in 300 ml/12 fl oz of water and bring to a simmer

Reduce the heat to low and cover the pan tightly. Cook very gently for at least 30 minutes, until the chicken is cooked through. Keep the heat low and turn over the pieces at least once during the cooking.

When the chicken is cooked, lift it from the pan and keep warm on a heated serving dish. Skim off any excess fat from the surface of the cooking liquid. Turn up the heat and boil until thickened and reduced by a quarter.

Adjust the seasoning. Pour in the crème fraîche, stir well and heat through. As soon as the sauce is piping hot, spoon it over the chicken. If you like, snip over a few leaves of fresh coriander. Serve as soon as possible.

EMINCE DE POULET AU MADERE

CHICKEN STRIPS WITH MADEIRA, HAM AND GREEN PEPPERCORNS

Emincer means to cut into thin long strips and is a popular technique in French cooking, both for reheating meat and for quickly cooking tender pieces of prime cut fillet in a light sauce.

★ Heat half the butter in a sauté pan. As soon as the butter starts to sizzle, tip in the chicken and stir for 2 to 3 minutes over a moderate heat. Roll each slice of ham into a cigarette shape and snip into the pan. Add the sage, peppercorns, Madeira and stock or water and soy sauce, stir well. Bring to a simmer, season lightly and reduce the heat a little.

Cover and cook gently for 10 to 12 minutes. Whisk in the cream then the rest of the butter. Adjust the seasoning and serve as soon as possible.

Serves 4

450 g/1 lb boned skinned
chicken breast, cut into
strips, about 2.5 cm/ 1 in
wide and no longer than
7.5 cm/3 in long
45 g/1½ oz chilled diced
butter
4 thin slices of dry-cured
ham, such as Bayonne,
Prosciutto or Serrano
3 fresh sage leaves, snipped
or 1 scant tsp dried
rubbed sage
1 tbsp drained green
peppercorns
5 tbsp Madeira
6 tbsp chicken stock (or
water mixed with 1 tsp light
soy sauce)
1 generous tbsp soured
cream, crème fraîche or
single cream
sea salt and freshly ground
black pepper

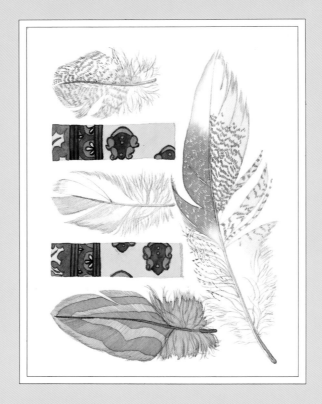

VOLAILLES EN MORCEAUX

POULTRY PIECES

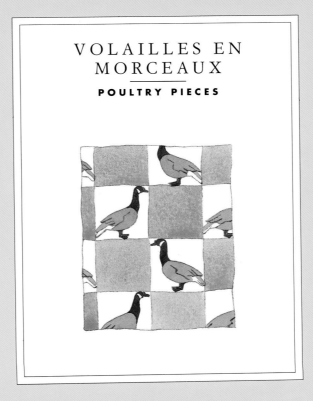

OIE EN DAUBE

GOOSE POT-ROAST

Serves 6

1 small goose, jointed
2 tsp oil
100 g/4 oz rindless smoked
streaky bacon, chopped and
blanched
15 g/½ oz butter
2 red onions, finely chopped
1 clove garlic, crushed
1 tbsp flour
6 juniper berries
400 ml/16 fl oz dry white
wine or a mixture of dry
white wine and water
1 small can tomatoes,
drained
1 bouquet garni
2 shallots, very finely
chopped
1 heaped tbsp finely grated
orange zest
2 tbsp finely snipped parsley
salt and freshly ground
black pepper

Goose and its unique fat dominate the cuisine of the south west of France. Somewhat more quietly perhaps, it also makes its presence felt at the opposite end of the country, in the north east. This recipe is based on a goose dish traditionally prepared in the Lorraine to celebrate Martinmas, the feast of St Martin, on 11 November.

★ Using paper towels, wipe a large sauté pan with oil. Sauté the bacon over moderate heat until golden. Season the goose and sauté for 15 to 20 minutes until browned, turning the pieces over several times and keeping the heat under control. Pour out any fat.

Melt in the butter, then scatter in the onions and garlic, and cook for a minute, stirring. Sprinkle over the flour, add the juniper berries and stir for a minute. Pour in the wine and top with just enough water to cover. Add the tomatoes and bouquet garni. Season lightly and bring to a simmer over moderate heat. Cover tightly, reduce the heat a little and simmer slowly for about 1½ to 1¾ hours. Stir a few times during cooking.

In a cup, mix the shallots, orange zest and parsley. Remove the bouquet garni from the pot. Adjust the seasoning. Sprinkle the dish with the shallot and orange mixture and serve while still hot.

MAGRETS DE CANARD AUX FRUITS ROUGES

DUCK BREASTS WITH RED WINE BERRY SAUCE

Vacuum-packed duck breasts, *magrets de canard sous vide*, are now widely available. Of all poultry cuts, these are most likely to please die-hard lovers of steak and red meat. Score the skin deeply before cooking to allow the plump cushion of fat under it to flavour and protect the delicate lean flesh.

★ With a sharp knife, score the skin side of the duck breasts, cutting into the flesh, several times in parallel lines. Season generously.

Place a heavy-based frying pan over high heat. Put the breasts in the hot pan, skin-side down. Cook for 10 to 12 minutes, reducing the heat a little towards the end.

Discard most of the fat. Turn over the duck breasts, reduce the heat and cover. Continue cooking for 4 to 6 minutes – the timing, as for red meats, will depend on how pink or well cooked you like your duck.

Put the breasts on a heated serving dish, cover and keep warm while you make the sauce.

Put the chopped shallots in the pan and sauté for 2 to 3 minutes over moderate heat. Moisten with the stock or water and soy sauce, stir until simmering, then add the mustard, berries, port (or orange juice and sherry vinegar) and return to a simmer, still stirring. Add the preserve and stir for a minute or two. Adjust the seasoning – add a little sugar if the sauce is not sweet enough. Whisk in the butter, if you like.

Slice the duck breasts – each will serve 2 people. Spoon the sauce over the slices and serve immediately.

Serves 4

2 boned duck breasts, each weighing about 300 to 350 g/10 to 12 oz
2 shallots, finely chopped
125 ml/4 fl oz chicken stock (or water and 2 tsp light soy sauce)
1 tsp hot Dijon mustard
4 tbsp red berries (ie blackcurrants, cranberries, redcurrants, blackberries), fresh or frozen
3 tbsp port or 1 tbsp sherry vinegar mixed with 2 tbsp orange juice
1 tbsp blackcurrant or similar preserve
sugar (optional)
15 g/½ oz chilled diced butter (optional)
sea salt and freshly ground black pepper

BLANQUETTE DE DINDE

TURKEY IN WHITE LEMON SAUCE

Serves 4

1 carrot, peeled and chopped
½ head of celery, trimmed and chopped
1 Spanish onion, chopped
bouquet garni
1 tsp dried thyme
3 strips of zest, 1 tbsp grated zest and 3 tbsp juice of unwaxed lemon
300 ml/12 fl oz dry white wine
700 g/1½ lb boned turkey breast, cut into large strips
125 g /5 oz button onions, peeled
125 g /5 oz button mushrooms, wiped and sliced
45 g/1½ oz chilled diced butter
1 tbsp cornflour
2 egg yolks
4 to 5 tbsp single cream
sea salt and freshly ground black pepper

White turkey breast is an excellent meat with which to make *blanquette*, the most pale-coloured and delicate of French casseroles. This recipe is a little on the long side, but it is not difficult and you can have a break before you finish the sauce. The end result is fragrant and subtle – a perfect dish for a supper party. Serve with rice or boiled potatoes.

★ Put the vegetables, bouquet garni, thyme and strips of lemon zest in a large sauté pan or cooking pot. Pour in the wine and add enough cold water to cover the vegetables and the turkey strips (when you add them later). Season and bring to a simmer. Cook over moderate heat for 15 to 20 minutes, skimming off foam and bits from the surface.

Season the strips of turkey and sprinkle with the grated lemon zest. Add to the pot, bring back to a gentle simmer and cook over low heat for 15 to 20 minutes, until tender, skimming if necessary.

Meanwhile, blanch the button onions for 5 minutes in lightly salted water, then drain and reserve. Sprinkle the mushrooms with a tablespoon of lemon juice and sauté for 3 to 5 minutes in a frying pan with a small piece of butter. Reserve on a double layer of paper towels.

Carefully strain most of the cooking liquid from the pan into a jug. Leave the turkey strips in the pan with a little liquid, discard the flavourings and cooking vegetables. Sprinkle in a tablespoon of lemon juice. Cover and keep warm. The dish can be left for a while at this stage.

VOLAILLES

OTHER POULTRY

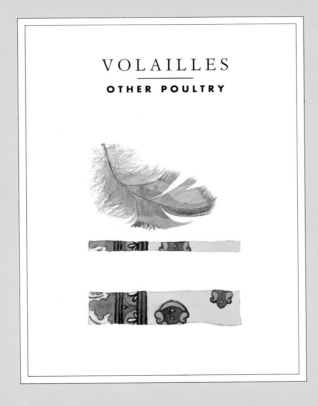

CANARD ROTI A L'ORANGE

ROAST DUCK WITH ORANGE SAUCE

Serves 4

*1 oven-ready duck, wiped
clean and at room
temperature
2 tbsp finely grated zest of
unwaxed orange
1 tbsp groundnut or
sunflower oil
2 tsp green peppercorns,
drained and crushed
2 tbsp brandy
2 tbsp Cointreau or other
orange liqueur
250 ml/8 fl oz freshly
squeezed orange juice
1 tbsp white wine or sherry
vinegar
1 heaped tsp cornflour
2 small juicy oranges, peeled,
pith removed and thinly
sliced (optional)
30 g/1 oz butter (optional)
sea salt and freshly ground
black pepper*

Duck is a fatty bird that reacts beautifully to being prepared with fruit – particularly sweetly acidic oranges. I cook my duck longer than most of my French friends and relatives; expect a bird with very crispy skin and a still moist but thoroughly cooked flesh.

★ Heat the oven to 220°C/425°F/Gas 7. In a cup mix together half the grated orange zest, oil and crushed green peppercorns. Season the mixture. Season the cavity of the duck and spoon in a tablespoon each of brandy and Cointreau. Using a pastry brush, paint the outside of the duck with the zest and oil mixture. Put the bird breast-side down on a rack in a roasting tin.

Roast for 30 minutes. Turn the duck breast-side up, baste and season again. Roast for 15 to 20 minutes then reduce the temperature to 160°C/325°F/Gas 3. Continue roasting for about 40 minutes, basting several times. At the end of roasting, the juices should run clear when you pierce the inside of the leg with a skewer. Sprinkle the rest of the brandy and Cointreau over the duck, tip the cooking juices from the roasting tin into a jug and leave the duck to settle for 10 minutes in the switched off oven. Stand the jug in cold water.

While the duck is settling, simmer the rest of the orange zest with the orange juice and vinegar together in a small saucepan for 5 minutes over moderate heat. Skim the top layer of fat from the jug and strain the rest of the cooking juices into the orange mixture. Heat until simmering, then stir in the cornflour. Cook for 2 to 3 minutes, still stirring.

If you like, sauté the orange slices in the butter over low heat for a minute or two. Arrange on a heated serving dish.

When carving the duck, collect all the juices and strain these into the sauce. Place the carved duck on a heated serving dish, on top of the orange slices, if using. Pour the sauce into a heated jug or sauce boat, adjust the seasoning and serve as soon as possible.

PINTADE AU CHOU

GUINEA FOWL AND CABBAGE POT-ROAST

Serves 4

1 plump guinea fowl or free range chicken, wiped and ready to cook
1 tbsp groundnut or sunflower oil
25 g/1 oz diced chilled butter
1 Savoy cabbage, cored, trimmed and quartered
100 g/4 oz diced smoked bacon, blanched
6 tbsp dry white wine
6 tbsp chicken stock or water mixed with 1 tsp light soy sauce
1 tsp dried ground thyme
sea salt and freshly ground black pepper

Guinea fowl is very popular in France and French-bred guinea fowls are exported all over the world. It tends to be a little on the dry side but, for a barnyard bird, it has a delicate, yet surprisingly gamey flavour which is well partnered here by Savoy cabbage.

★   Lightly season the guinea fowl inside and outside. Blanch the cabbage for 5 minutes in plenty of lightly salted boiling water. Drain well in a colander.

In a deep sauté pan or flame-proof cooking pot, heat the oil and half the butter. Add the guinea fowl and brown over a moderate heat for 15 to 20 minutes, turning it gradually so that it colours evenly. Reduce the heat a little if the bird is browning too fast.

Remove from the pot and reserve. Wipe the pan with paper towels. Scatter in the bacon and stir over moderate heat for 2 minutes until golden.

Put the drained cabbage quarters in the pot. Place the guinea fowl in the centre. Sprinkle with the thyme, moisten with the wine and stock or water. Season lightly. Cover tightly and cook for at least 1 hour, until the guinea fowl is cooked through.

To serve, lift the guinea fowl, cabbage and bacon from the pot, letting the juices drip back in. Turn up the heat under the pot and bring to the boil. Leave to reduce a little.

Arrange the cabbage and bacon on a heated serving dish. Keep warm while you joint the bird and place it on the cabbage. Whisk the rest of the butter into the reduced cooking liquid, adjust the seasoning and spoon over the guinea fowl and cabbage.

CANETON AUX OLIVES

DUCKLING WITH OLIVES

Serves 4

*1 oven-ready duckling,
wiped clean and at room
temperature
1 tbsp olive oil
30 g/1 oz chilled diced butter
250 ml/8 fl oz dry white
wine, plus extra, if needed
½ tsp each dried ground
thyme and marjoram
1 large Spanish onion,
finely chopped
1 clove garlic, crushed
450 g/1 lb ripe tomatoes,
blanched, seeded, skinned
and chopped, or a large can
of tomatoes, drained
180 g/6 oz stoned
green olives
sea salt and freshly ground
black pepper*

Season the duckling well inside and out with salt and freshly ground black pepper.

In a large flame-proof cooking pot, heat the oil with a third of the butter. Sauté the duckling over moderate heat for about 15 minutes, turning it gradually until the skin is crisp and golden all over. Keep an eye on the heat and do not let the duck blacken.

Lift out the duckling and put on a plate. Discard the fat, reserving 2 tablespoons to put in a frying pan. Return the duckling to the pot, add the wine and herbs to the pot, bring to a simmer, then cover tightly and reduce the heat. Cook gently for about 30 minutes, basting the duckling once or twice.

Meanwhile sauté the onion, garlic and tomatoes in the reserved fat over a low heat for 8 to 10 minutes, stirring occasionally until softened.

Stir the onion and tomato mixture into the pot, then cover and simmer as before for a further 30 minutes.

Stir in the olives, adding a little wine or water if the mixture looks too dry. Cover and simmer over low heat for 20 minutes.

Joint the duckling and keep warm. Stir the rest of the butter into the olive mixture. Adjust the seasoning. Return the duckling to the pot and serve very hot.

POUSSINS BASQUAISE

POUSSIN CASSEROLE WITH SWEET PEPPERS

More often than not dishes *à la basquaise*, from France's Basque province, at the south west corner of the country, include sweet peppers, tomatoes and the dry cured ham of the region, *jambon de Bayonne*. This recipe is no exception.

★ Using strong kitchen scissors, cut the poussins in half lengthways. Season generously with paprika, salt and pepper. Heat half the oil in a large sauté pan or cooking pot wide enough to take the poussin halves side by side. Brown the poussins for 10 minutes over moderate heat, stirring and turning so that they colour evenly. Lift from the pot and reserve.

Add the rest of the oil to the pot. Sauté the onion and garlic for a few minutes over moderate heat, then return the poussins (and their juices) to the pot. Stir for a minute, then pour in the wine and sprinkle over half the parsley. Season again and bring to a simmer.

Reduce the heat a little, cover and cook for 20 minutes, then add the tomatoes, sweet peppers and ham. Cover again and continue cooking gently for about 30 minutes, until the poussins are cooked through.

Just before serving, adjust the seasoning and sprinkle over the rest of the parsley. Serve from the pot.

Serves 4

2 plump poussins, wiped
½ tsp paprika
3 tbsp olive oil
1 large sweet white onion,
finely chopped
1 clove garlic, crushed
125 ml/4 fl oz dry
white wine
2 tbsp finely snipped
fresh parsley
450 g/1 lb tomatoes,
blanched, seeded, skinned
and chopped or 1 large can
tomatoes, drained
2 sweet red peppers, charred,
skinned, cored and seeded
2 thin slices dry-cured ham,
rolled and snipped into strips
salt and freshly ground
black pepper

COQUELET GRILLE A LA DIABLE

GRILLED POUSSIN WITH A HOT SHALLOT SAUCE

Serves 2

1 poussin
30 g/1 oz soft butter
1 tsp Dijon or coarse-grain mustard
2 tsp fresh breadcrumbs
sea salt and freshly ground black pepper

For the sauce diable:

2 shallots, finely chopped
15 g/½ oz chilled diced butter
4 tbsp white wine vinegar
5 tbsp white wine
5 tbsp chicken stock or water mixed with 1 tsp light soy sauce
cayenne pepper
1 tbsp finely snipped fresh parsley

Not as devilishly hot as other variations on the *diable* theme, this dish is pleasantly piquant. The poussins are good enough grilled this way to be served on their own, but the sauce adds a more-ish *je-ne-sais-quoi* and is worth trying with other poultry and light meats.

★ Heat the grill to high. Using strong kitchen scissors, cut the poussin in half lengthways. Press to flatten and season generously. Spread with half the soft butter. Grill breast-side up for 10 minutes, then turn over and grill for 15 minutes, reducing the heat a little. Turn back up and grill for a further 10 to 15 minutes, basting well with the cooking juices, until the poussin is cooked through. Reduce the heat still further if the skin shows signs of burning.

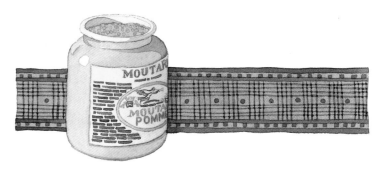

Prepare the sauce while the poussin is grilling. In a saucepan, sauté the shallots with half the diced butter over low heat. Add the vinegar, wine, stock or water and season lightly. Bring to a simmer and cook for 10 minutes without covering. Keep an eye on the heat and stir a few times.

In a cup, mix the mustard and breadcrumbs. Swirl the rest of the soft butter over the poussin, then spread over the mustard mixture. Grill for a few minutes until golden and bubbly.

Just before serving, spoon the cooking juices into the sauce. Whisk in half the parsley and the rest of the chilled butter. Add a touch of cayenne pepper and adjust the seasoning. Sprinkle the rest of the parsley over the poussin. Serve hot, with the sauce.

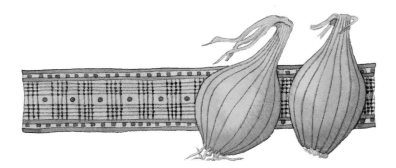

ROTI DE BLANC DE DINDE FARCI

STUFFED TURKEY BREAST JOINT

Serves 4 to 6

a boned and tied turkey breast joint weighing about 700 g/1½ lb
butter and olive oil for greasing
1 large Spanish onion, finely chopped
2 large carrots, peeled and chopped
300 g/10 oz small mushrooms, wiped and thinly sliced
1 clove garlic, crushed
½ tsp each dried sage, thyme and oregano
45 g/1½ oz chilled diced butter
300 ml/10 fl oz dry white wine mixed with stock or with water and 1 tsp soy sauce
1 tbsp finely snipped fresh herbs (parsley, chives or chervil)
sea salt and freshly ground black pepper

Turkey does not seriously compete with chicken in the French poultry popularity charts, but, in recent years, it has acquired a better image. Free-range baby turkeys, *dindonneaux*, are bred with great care all over the country. The stuffing and the mushroom-flavoured sauce in the following recipe are a (very loose) tribute to a stuffed roast I much enjoyed as a child, *veau Orloff*.

★ Prepare the stuffing. Process together the garlic, shallots, sage, thyme, oregano and strips of ham for a few seconds. Scrape the mixture off the sides of the bowl. Season, then add the olive oil and cheese. Whizz until smoothly blended.

Using a sharp knife, cut the turkey into medium-thick slices, carefully stopping about two thirds of the way down. Work between the pieces of string, taking care not to cut them. Spread the stuffing between the partly cut slices. Insert 2 or 3 skewers crossways into the turkey to help keep it together.

Heat the oven to 200°C/400°F/Gas 6. Generously grease a roasting tin or gratin dish with butter and olive oil. Spread the onion and carrots in the pan. Season and scatter over the sliced mushrooms, crushed garlic and dried herbs. Place the turkey on top. Dot with half the chilled butter and roast for about 30 minutes.

Pour the wine and stock over the turkey, baste well. Reduce the heat to 190°C/375°F/Gas 5 and roast for another hour, until the turkey is cooked through. Baste several times during cooking and reduce the heat a little if the turkey looks too hot and dry.

Leave the turkey to settle for 10 minutes in the turned off oven. Meanwhile, put the cooking juices and vegetables into a blender or food processor. Blend and pour into a small saucepan. Dilute with a little extra stock and wine if the mixture looks too thick (or if you don't think there is enough of it). Heat through gently. Whisk in the rest of the chilled butter. Adjust the seasoning.

To serve, put the turkey on a heated serving dish. Remove the skewers and string and finish slicing. Spoon over the sauce. Sprinkle with the fresh herbs and serve as soon as possible.

For the stuffing:

1 clove garlic, crushed
2 shallots, chopped
¼ tsp each dried sage, thyme and oregano
1 slice of dry-cured ham, chopped
2 tbsp olive oil
75 g/3 oz cream cheese or mild fresh goat's cheese, crumbled

Heat the rest of the butter in a saucepan, add the flour and stir for a minute to make a pale roux – take off the heat before it has time to colour. Pour the cooking liquid into the roux, and bring to a boil, stirring vigorously. Simmer gently for a few minutes, stirring frequently, until smooth and thickened.

Beat the yolks in a bowl and stir in 3 tablespoons of hot sauce then the cream. Pour this mixture into the saucepan, and stir over low heat until blended.

Pour the sauce over the turkey strips and stir in the mushrooms and onions. Cook over low heat until heated through. Sprinkle in the rest of the lemon juice, adjust the seasoning and serve hot.

CUISSES DE POULET A LA MOUTARDE

CHICKEN THIGHS IN A MUSTARD SAUCE

Serves 4

8 skinned and boned chicken thighs, or 6-8 rabbit pieces
1 tbsp oil
30 g/1 oz butter
1 tbsp dried ground thyme
1 red onion, finely chopped
2 shallots, finely chopped
½ clove garlic, crushed
1 tbsp flour
3 tbsp hot French mustard
(coarse-grain or Dijon)
175 ml/6 fl oz dry white
wine mixed with stock or
water and 2 tsp soy sauce
1½ tbsp brandy
4 tbsp crème fraîche
1 tbsp finely snipped chives
sea salt and freshly ground
black pepper

This dish is classically prepared using rabbit. However, chicken thighs are an excellent alternative, as my bunny-shy friends will testify. Serve with boiled new potatoes.

★   Heat the oil and butter in a sauté pan and sauté the onion, shallots and garlic for a few minutes over moderate heat. Season the chicken pieces and sprinkle them with the flour and thyme.

Add to the pan and sauté for a few minutes over moderate heat, turning the pieces over so that they cook evenly. Reduce the heat a little as soon as the meat has browned.

Stir in the wine and stock, and a tablespoon of mustard. Bring to a simmer, then reduce the heat, cover and cook for about 40 minutes until the chicken is tender. Stir from time to time and keep the heat low.

Sprinkle in the brandy and stir. Lift the meat and onion mixture from the pan and keep warm on a heated serving dish while you finish the sauce.

Add the crème fraîche and the rest of the mustard to the pan. Stir over low heat until hot and blended into the cooking liquor. Adjust the seasoning. Spoon the sauce over the chicken. Sprinkle with the chives and serve as soon as possible.

GIBELOTTE ROGER

POACHER'S POULTRY STEW

A gibelotte is a country stew based on game birds, *gibier à plume*. In time-honoured French style, I poached this recipe off a friend, Roger Demoiselles, a good cook who comes from northern Brittany.

★ Season the flour, mix in the herbs and pat into the meat pieces. Heat the oil in a sauté pan, sauté the shallots and garlic over moderate heat for 2 to 3 minutes.

Add the floured meat and sauté until golden, turning the pieces over so that they colour evenly. Add the wine and the tomatoes. Season with a touch of cayenne and paprika. Bring to a simmer, then reduce the heat a little and cook, uncovered, for about 35 minutes – the cooking liquid will thicken and reduce. Cover and leave until cold, then leave in a cold place for a few hours or refrigerate overnight.

Sauté the bacon in a frying pan with the butter over moderate heat until crisp. Lift from the pan and reserve. Add the mushrooms to the pan, season and sauté for a few minutes.

Stir the mushrooms into the stew. Place over low heat and bring to a simmer. Leave to simmer gently for about 15 minutes, stirring a few times.

Just before serving, stir in the crème fraîche and bacon. Heat through, then sprinkle with parsley and serve immediately.

Serves 4

4 to 6 skinned rabbit pieces,
rinsed and wiped, or 8
skinned chicken thighs
1 tbsp flour
$\frac{1}{2}$ tsp each dried ground
thyme and marjoram or
sweet savoury
2 tbsp olive oil
3 shallots, finely chopped
2 cloves garlic, crushed
550 ml/1 pt dry white wine
1 large can chopped tomatoes
cayenne
paprika
2 slices rindless streaky
smoked bacon, blanched and
chopped
15 g/$\frac{1}{2}$ oz butter
350 g/12 oz button
mushrooms, wiped and
sliced
2 to 3 tbsp crème fraîche,
cream or low fat crème
fraîche
1 heaped tbsp finely snipped
parsley
sea salt and freshly ground
black pepper

A MANGER FROID

THREE COLD POULTRY DISHES

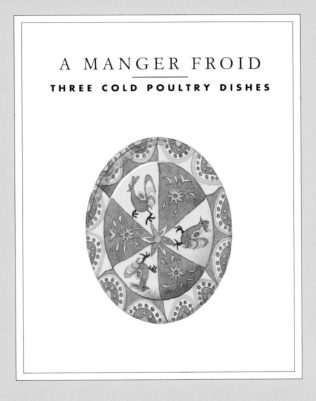

CHAUD-FROID DE POULET A L'ESTRAGON

POACHED COLD CHICKEN IN CREAMY WHITE ASPIC

Serves 4

4 top of the range chicken supremes (boned or part-boned chicken breasts)
½ Spanish onion, chopped
bouquet garni
several sprigs of tarragon
3 to 4 strips and 2 tbsp juice of an unwaxed lemon
4 black peppercorns
200 ml/8 fl oz dry white wine
40 g/1½ oz butter
40 g/1½ oz plain flour
100 ml/4 fl oz thick cream
two 25 g/1 oz sachets good quality aspic powder
2 tbsp Madeira, port or orange juice
sea salt and freshly ground black pepper

T his recipe is just what it says: it consists of chicken (*poulet*) prepared hot (*chaud*) and served cold (*froid*). It looks impressive, tastes delicate, requires no last minute preparation, and is easy to serve.

★ Prepare the dish the day before the meal. In a large sauté pan, put the onion with the bouquet garni, a few sprigs of tarragon, the lemon zest, and peppercorns. Pour in the white wine, then top up with cold water; you will need enough liquid to cover the chicken supremes. Season, bring to a simmer, and cook over moderate heat for 20 minutes.

Add the supremes, return to the boil and immediately reduce the heat. Simmer gently for 30 to 40 minutes, or until the supremes are cooked through. Skim off any surface dirt and keep an eye on the heat. Lift the supremes from the pan and drain well. Leave until cool enough to handle, then remove the skin.

Strain the cooking liquid through a lined muslin sieve into a measuring jug. Reserve to make the sauce.

Melt the butter in a saucepan. Add the flour and cook for 40 seconds over moderate heat, stirring vigorously to make a pale roux. Whisk in about 300 ml/12 fl oz cooking liquid, and bring to a simmer, whisking steadily. Reduce the heat a fraction and simmer gently for 8 to 10 minutes, stirring from time to time. Adjust the seasoning. If there are lumps in the mixture, push it through a fine sieve. Leave to cool a little, stirring occasionally.

Whisk in the cream and lemon juice.

Make about 200 ml/8 fl oz liquid aspic, using leftover cooking liquid and one entire sachet of powder, but otherwise following the instructions on the packet.

Whisk the liquid aspic into the creamy white sauce, strain through a fine sieve into a clean bowl and leave to get gold and syrupy. Dry the supremes with paper towels. Place them over a cooling rack on top of a platter. Using a large spoon, coat the supremes with the thickened sauce. Save all the leftover sauce. Refrigerate the supremes for 2 hours or until set. Repeat the coating process – you will need to reheat the solidified sauce to return it to a syrup-like working consistency. Refrigerate the supremes overnight.

The next day, at least $2^{1}/_{2}$ hours before serving, use the other sachet of aspic powder to make up more aspic. This time follow exactly the instructions, flavouring the liquid aspic with a little Madeira, port or orange juice.

Arrange a few pretty sprigs of tarragon and chives on the supremes. Using the cooling rack and the same method as before, coat the supremes with syrupy aspic – this will make the *chaud-froid* glisten. Refrigerate until set. Chill the leftover aspic and cut into dice before serving.

Serve the supremes on an attractive dish, garnish with chopped aspic and pretty sprigs of tarragon.

PETITE TERRINE DE FOIES DE VOLAILLE

CHICKEN LIVER MOUSSE

Serves 4-6

550 g/1¼ lb chicken livers, trimmed, washed and patted dry
3 tbsp brandy
6 tbsp port
1 tbsp oil
1 bay leaf
½ tsp each dried ground sage and thyme
nutmeg
65 g/2½ oz butter
2 shallots, finely chopped
white parts of 3 large spring onions, finely chopped
sea salt and freshly ground black pepper

This smooth chicken liver mousse has a deep flavour and is very good served with buttered toast, and better still, with sweet toasted brioche.

★ Put the prepared chicken livers in a bowl with the brandy, port, oil, bay leaf, sage and thyme. Season with pepper and a touch of nutmeg. Mix well, then cover and refrigerate overnight.

Heat the butter in a frying pan. Add the shallots and spring onions, season and sauté for 3 minutes over moderate heat, stirring a few times. Reduce the heat to very low.

Drain the chicken livers, reserving the marinade juices. Discard the bay leaf. Add the livers to the pan and sauté over moderate heat for 10 minutes, stirring constantly. Reduce the heat after a few minutes.

Leave the cooked livers to cool a little, then put in the food processor with the marinade. Whizz until very smooth.

Adjust the seasoning – the mousse should be well flavoured. Spoon into a suitable earthenware dish (for instance a rectangular butter dish or a small soufflé dish), spread in smoothly and knock against the work top to settle the contents. Leave until cold, then cover and refrigerate overnight before serving.

MOUSSE MINUTE DE FOIES DE VOLAILLE AUX CHAMPIGNONS

QUICK CHICKEN LIVER MOUSSE WITH MUSHROOMS

Serves 4 to 6

100 g/4 oz bought chicken liver pâté
125 g/5 oz small brown mushrooms, wiped and very thinly sliced
45 g/1½ oz butter
2 tbsp cream cheese
1 tbsp port
1 tsp brandy
a few drops of Worcestershire sauce or 1 tsp crushed green peppercorns (optional)

My current favourite quick way of quietly improving bland chicken liver pâté. In feebler moments, I have passed off the whole preparation as my own creation – much to my husband's amusement.

★   In a frying pan sauté the mushrooms with a knob of butter over moderate heat for a few minutes. Dry with paper towels to absorb excess moisture.

Cut the pâté into small pieces. Put in the food processor with the sautéed mushrooms. Whizz until smooth, scrape from the sides of the bowl, then add the rest of the butter, the cream cheese, port and brandy.

Taste and adjust the seasoning. If you like, stir in a few drops of Worcestershire sauce and a few crushed green peppercorns. Refrigerate for at least 20 minutes or longer still if possible. The mousse will keep for a couple of days in the refrigerator.

LIST OF RECIPES